Christmas
in Italy

Christmas in Italy

Corinne Ross

PASSPORT BOOKS
a division of *NTC Publishing Group*
Lincolnwood, Illinois USA

This edition first published in 1991 by Passport Books, a division of NTC Publishing Group,
4255 West Touhy Avenue, Lincolnwood (Chicago), Illinois 60646-1975 U.S.A.
© 1974 by World Book, Inc. All rights reserved. No part
of this book may be reproduced, stored in a retrieval
system, or transmitted in any form, or by any means,
electronic, mechanical, photocopying or otherwise,
without the prior permission of NTC Publishing Group.
Manufactured in Hong Kong.

1 2 3 4 5 6 7 8 9 LR 9 8 7 6 5 4 3 2

Contents

Christmas really began in Italy. Christ was born in the tiny village of Bethlehem, in Judea. But His birthday was first celebrated in Rome almost 300 years later, when Emperor Constantine adopted the new faith of Christianity.

Church leaders in those times often substituted saints for pagan gods and Christian holy days for pagan celebrations. No one knows for certain, even today, the exact date of Christ's birth. The feast day of the Romans' old pagan god Mithras, however, fell on December 25, and that was the day chosen to honor Christ.

The period between mid-December and early January had long been one of almost nonstop revelry in ancient Rome. It began with the Saturnalia, a winter solstice festival, and ended with the Roman New Year, the Calends. It was a joyous time of good will and sharing. People exchanged visits and gave gifts, especially at New Year's. Candles and clay dolls were favorite presents; dates, figs, honey, and coins were also popular. Laurel branches were given as gifts, too, and used to decorate houses and temples.

Italy at Christmastime

After the coming of Christianity, the season became a time of holiness, of reverence for Christ. Instead of ending at New Year's, it extended to January 6, when the Three Kings were believed to have reached Bethlehem. They gave their gifts to the Infant Jesus on that day, and so the Romans, too, began to exchange presents on Epiphany.

Christmas in Italy today is still very much a religious holiday. The season begins with a novena, a nine-day period of special church services ending on Christmas Eve. Lots of Christmas trees may be seen nowadays in Italy, but the real focal point of Christmas observances is the Nativity scene.

The mangers range from simple, homemade re-creations of the old Bible story to elaborate displays containing hundreds of pieces and dozens of different scenes. The tiny image of the Christ Child in His crib is deeply cherished by Italians, and the country is literally studded with Nativity scenes at Christmastime. Presents are often placed near the manger, and families pray together in front of it.

Important as religion is to most Italians, however, the Christmas season is not devoted only to church-going and prayer. Children put on plays in school, give recitations, and make decorations. Families make special trips to the colorful Christmas markets to buy presents and new manger figures. Window shopping is great fun—stores and streets are all gaily decorated with lights and Christmas greenery.

The opera season opens in December, too, and nowadays those who can afford it go on ski vacations. In Sicily, puppet shows are a holiday tradition, with large, hand-carved puppets acting out fairy tales and legendary battles.

Christmas Eve and Christmas Day are strictly family affairs. There's an old saying that goes: "You can spend New Year's with anyone you choose, but Christmas is for family." December 26, St. Stephen's Day, was once a day of religious devotion. Now it is mostly one of rest or visiting. People call on friends and relatives, bringing gifts and sharing holiday foods. And they go to see some of the many marvelous manger displays.

Fresh snow blankets the trees and ground as churchgoers in northern Italy head home after Christmas morning services (left). One of Italy's many manger scenes, this lifelike tableau has been set up on the Piazza Navona in Rome (above). Mary and Joseph, along with oxen and sheep, keep watch over the Infant Jesus as shepherds approach to worship the newborn Babe.

New Year's Eve is celebrated with parties, dancing, champagne, and fireworks. Shortly after New Year's children return to school, but the end of the Christmas season does not actually come until Epiphany, January 6.

Italy is a land of diverse regions, a narrow country shaped somewhat like a boot. It stretches almost 1,000 miles, from the snow-covered Alps to sunbaked Sicily. Actually, Sicily is an island; on a map, it is the football the boot is about to kick. Sardinia, another island, lies northwest of Sicily, about 135 miles west of Rome.

In the mountain provinces of Italy Christmases are cold, with lots of ice and snow. In Rome, the holidays may be touched by a hint of springlike weather. More likely, it will be chilly and damp. In the south, midwinter days are usually warm and sunshiny.

Christmas customs are just as varied as the weather; even within a particular region they are not always the same. Gift giving, for instance, occurs on a whole raft of different days.

On December 6, Saint Nicholas' feast day, the saint visits many of the children of Bari and other towns along the Adriatic coast. Nicholas was Archbishop of Myra in Asia Minor in the fourth century. Legend says that his remains were stolen in 1087 by a band of Italian clergy and merchants. They carried them to Bari, in the region of Apulia, Italy, and there a shrine was built in Nicholas' honor. A

Lit with glowing candles, this gilt ceppo, *a three-tiered pyramid, holds a tiny manger scene on its bottom shelf. The other shelves are bedecked with greenery, ornaments, and more small manger figures.*

festival is held each year on his day, and thousands of people make pilgrimages to his tomb.

In Sicily, Santa Lucia brings presents on her day, December 13. Like Saint Nicholas, she lived in the fourth century. Poor Lucia was condemned to death, some say because she refused the attentions of a wicked nobleman. Others believe it was because she staunchly defended her unpopular Christmas beliefs. Lucia, accompanied by a donkey carrying baskets of gifts, goes about her rounds wearing a blue, star-sprinkled cloak. Youngsters place their shoes outside the door the night before, hoping to find them well filled in the morning. Boys and girls sometimes place food outdoors, too—for the donkey.

The custom of exchanging gifts at Christmas had already begun to be practiced in Italy when World War II came along. The American G.I.'s who were stationed there reinforced the custom. They brought Santa Claus (not to be confused with Italy's Saint Nicholas) and often decorated Christmas trees, too.

Christmas trees today are very popular, especially in northern regions. Most are imported from northern Europe, but many families prefer an artificial tree—it lasts longer. Others buy live, potted trees, which not only survive better but can be replanted. Southern Italians sometimes decorate a tree with fresh fruit and foil-covered chocolates. Children love these trees because on January 6 they are allowed to eat the trimmings.

The square in front of the cathedral in Milan is always popular with pigeons. Here they have joined Santa Claus and a young friend for a holiday picture.

In some regions, New Year's is another time for gifts, just as it was in ancient Rome. Long ago, a Yule log called a *ceppo* was dragged in from the woods and set afire with much ceremony. Often the children were blindfolded, and they would hit the log with sticks or tongs, causing sparks to fly up. When the blindfolds were removed, a pile of gifts would magically have appeared for each child. The ashes of the burned log were kept as a charm against storms.

Later the ceppo changed its shape, becoming a wood or cardboard pyramid with several shelves. It is gilded or covered with colored, fringed paper, and candles are attached to the sides. Gilded cherubs, pine cones, stars, birds, and other ornaments are added as decoration. One shelf holds the family's manger scene; others are for presents and perhaps a few family treasures.

Despite the growing trend toward giving gifts at Christmas, a large number of families still save their presents for Epiphany. Youngsters believe that a kindly old witch, *La Befana*, delivers the goodies. Even children who have received their real gifts on Christmas will get something on January 6 — perhaps a stocking filled with candy.

In large cities like Rome and Milan, Epiphany is the favorite day of traffic policemen. They are showered with offerings from motorists who understand the value of insurance. Mountains of gifts pile up around the police officer's stand, including bottles of wine, food or fruit baskets, and, sometimes, even a small car.

Giving gifts to policemen is a practical gesture, but Italians are also a superstitious people, and legends abound concerning the holidays. New Year's is the day on which you should try to do all your favorite things, so that you can go on doing them all year. It is also the time for forecasting the future. Young girls burn olive leaves to find out whom they will marry, or they toss slippers over their shoulders at a door. If the slipper ends up pointing toward the outside, its owner will be married within the year.

The first person you meet on New Year's Day is very important, too. A strong, stalwart male, especially a sailor, is considered good luck. But if you meet a child, you might die young. A priest is even worse, he means a funeral — maybe yours. And meeting a woman first is a disaster. Still today there are some seemingly sophisticated people who will not speak to a woman, even over the phone, first thing on January 1.

Epiphany is believed by many to be a time of wondrous happenings. Trees are suddenly covered with fruit, rivers and streams turn to gold, fountains flow with honey, and animals talk. In some regions, bonfires are kindled on Epiphany Eve. The direction in which the smoke blows indicates the weather for the New Year.

Italy is a vibrant, exciting place to be at Christmastime. In Rome, at sunset on Christmas Eve, cannons boom from the Castle of St. Angelo, announcing the start of the holy season. A few hours later, the city's streets are jammed with crowds heading for one of its more than 400 churches. At St. Peter's, the Pope himself conducts the Midnight Mass.

Way up in the snowy north of Italy, in Cortina D'Ampezzo, a spectacular event is held on Christmas Eve. It is called the *Fiaccolate degli Sciatori*. At midnight, the Alpine guides, holding flaming torches, ski down the mountainside. Darting over the slopes in sweeping curves and crisscross patterns, the skiers look like a giant cloud of fireflies flashing across the night.

New Year's Eve in most cities is celebrated with dazzling displays of fireworks. They are usually not planned civic events, but handheld, individual shows from rooftops, balconies, and street corners. Although firecrackers are illegal, and highly dangerous, the authorities find it difficult to enforce the law.

The noise made by swooshing rockets and bursting firecrackers is, however, only the beginning. Many joyful celebrants shoot guns, sometimes with live ammunition. And—especially in Naples—the night is made even livelier by the sound of many objects crashing to the sidewalk from windows above.

Neapolitans hurl just about anything—preferably breakable items—from their windows: bottles, pots and pans, old clothes, bicycles, furniture, even a bathtub or two. All this sound and fury goes back to the days when evil spirits were believed to be abroad at this time of the year. Fire—and lots of noise—scared the demons away.

A gigantic white ox leads a parade through the streets of Bologna on New Year's Eve. It is the procession of the *bue grasso,* the fat ox. The animal is decorated from his giant horns to his tail with multicolored ribbons and flowers. The procession ends just before midnight at the square of San Petronio. From a nearby hill a cannon roars, the great clock in the square strikes twelve, and thousands of onlookers light candles. Then fireworks light up the sky. In their midst a white flag appears. It is printed with the winning lottery number, and some lucky person has won the ox.

Children admire a magnificent manger scene with life-sized figures set in a volcanic cave in Acireale, Sicily.

Abbondanza! That is Italian for "abundance," or "plenty." And Italy's fabulous Christmas markets certainly seem to have an abundance of everything! You can find practically any item you want, and a thousand things you do not.

Early in December, tables and wooden stalls in vast numbers appear in the central squares of towns large and small. They spread out into side streets, too, many of which are closed to automobile traffic for the season. Happy, jostling crowds wander about looking, sometimes buying, playing games of chance, and eating. The markets are really more like carnivals: noisy, gaudy, and gay.

Let us take a tour of some typical markets, beginning with Milan's sprawling Sant'Ambrogio Fair. Like the others, it offers a marvelous variety of wares for sale: manger figures, Christmas ornaments and toys, clothes, and gifts. Vendors cry the merits of all manner of used goods, too, from incomplete sets of dishes to chipped Caruso records and "antiques" of recent vintage. Doorknobs and copper pans, old books and maps, even beat-up sewing machines and typewriters, rugs, more-or-less usable furniture, pictures, and mirrors are optimistically offered to browsing strollers.

The Christmas markets

Artists may be seen rapidly sketching caricatures or hopefully showing off their landscapes and religious paintings. Balloon sellers hawk their wares, a favorite balloon shape being the rabbit. Children toss balls or rings as they attempt to knock down rows of figures in game booths. The lucky winners can take home a stuffed animal — maybe a teddy bear. Bands of roving musicians, always a part of any Italian fair, fill the air with bouncy music.

Booths and pushcarts do a brisk business in flowers. Poinsettias, cyclamens, azaleas, and violets bloom in colorful profusion everywhere. Bunches of holly and mistletoe wrapped in cellophane, all ready to hang on doors, are also big sellers.

Things to eat — on the spot or to take home — tempt shoppers at every turn. The chestnut vendor has lots of customers; his stove is a good place to warm up chilled fingers. A popular Christmastime snack is a sandwich made with a slice of *porchetta*. This is a whole pigskin, complete with the head, stuffed with meat and roasted on an open fire. Countless stalls offer Christmas candy, chocolate, gum drops, licorice, nougats, and many other kinds. Others sell dried fruit and nuts, and sticky cones of spun sugar.

Food shop owners on the streets near the market vie with the open-air booths for attention by creating marvelous window displays. Pastry shops present trays of delectable cakes and cookies, good-smelling breads, and brightly wrapped boxes of *panettone*, Italy's traditional Christmas cake. Rabbits, capons, turkeys, and hams hang in the butcher's window, bedecked with greenery.

Italy's Christmas decorations are full of surprises. Here, two gaily costumed pigs reading a book are on display outside a butcher's shop (above top). *Tempting apples, pears, peaches, and other fruits adorn a store window in Milan* (below). *Realistic though they appear, all the fruits are actually candy, cleverly formed from marzipan and tinted by hand.*

A spectacular nighttime scene, this is the famous Christmas market in Rome's historic Piazza Navona. Crowds of people wander through the huge square, past long rows of booths overflowing with goods of all kinds.

17

Next door there is an enticing selection of salami, prosciutto, and *capicolli,* big spiced sausages. Then an irresistible mountain of cheese catches the eye, or maybe an arrangement of fruit: pears, strawberries, apricots, oranges, and apples. They appear so real one has to look twice to see that they are made of marzipan. Real fruit is sold, too, of course, set out in beautiful, gleaming pyramids.

In Venice, Florence, and Rome, huge wholesale fish markets open their doors to the public just for a day or so before Christmas. People stand, patiently waiting, until the official ceremonies are over. Then the markets become scenes of frantic activity as last-minute shoppers haggle with vendors over the prices of live eels and other fishy purchases.

Candy dolls in a charming assortment of guises are a tradition in Palermo's December market. Bologna's bustling Santa Lucia Market is set up under the portals of the Gothic Church of Santa Maria dei Servi. And Naples holds torchlight parades and fireworks displays in the Fondaco di San Gregorio Armeno, a small square near the waterfront.

One of the noisiest, gayest, most picturesque markets of all is held in Rome's Piazza Navona, beginning around December 15. The huge, historic square was once a center for ancient Roman holiday revelry. Chariot races took place there; it was even converted into a lake for small-scale naval battles. Today, three impressive fountains adorn the center of the piazza. Hundreds of kiosks, all jammed tightly together, are set up in long rows down the sides. Their roofs are painted in bright colors—orange and blue, red, yellow and green—rainbow stripes offering a cheerful contrast to the gloomy gray of the winter.

There is a large outdoor Nativity scene, too, which attracts thousands of visitors. Shortly before Christmas the Auxiliary Bishop of Rome appears on the balcony of the Braschi Palace overlooking the piazza. He blesses the square, then comes down and walks its entire length, accompanied by a retinue of clergy and civil dignitaries.

When they reach the manger they offer prayers, and the display is declared officially open. It is erected by the municipality of Rome; each year a different artist is entrusted with its design. On the year of the moon landing it portrayed a moonscape, Earth, and the three astronauts. Another year, the scene consisted of a huge bubble with carved figures representing Joseph, Mary, and the Christ Child.

On the last night of the fair, January 5—the eve of Epiphany—the Piazza Navona swarms with shoppers. It seems as though all of Rome descends upon this one square. Thousands of people mill about: tourists, Italian families en masse, couples out for an evening's entertainment, individuals of all sorts.

Merchants offer alluring bargains, hoping to sell out before tearing down their booths. Shoppers and sightseers good-naturedly push their way through the crowded aisles. Parents search for one last toy and, quite often, a lost child. Pretty girls pretend to ignore the flirtatious attentions of handsome, dark-eyed youths.

Children race through the swirling mass, yelling and setting up an earsplitting racket with toy whistles and trumpets. Withered grandmothers in black dicker fiercely with loudly shrieking vendors; old men and young wave their arms as they bellow greetings to friends. The musicians increase their decibel rate in happy competitions, and the din becomes deafening. It is a cheerful madhouse, exhausting and fun—and an absolutely essential element of the Roman holidays.

All Italian Christmas markets have at least one balloon vendor, and Milan's Sant' Ambrogio is no exception (above top). No matter how many manger figures one might have accumulated over the years, there is always room for one more (below).

It is the eve of Epiphany, the night of magic — when anything can happen. It is terribly hard for children to go to sleep on this night. But now they are tucked snugly in bed, dreaming of the exciting morning to come. Stockings, empty and waiting, hang by the fire. Everything is quiet; the house is very still.

Across the dark winter sky a strange figure flies like the wind. For a brief moment it is silhouetted against the moon. The figure pauses in its flight, then dives swiftly earthward. Whoosh! Down the chimney it pops. Quickly, it checks to make certain the children are sound asleep. Reassured, it cackles happily as it fills the stockings from a bulging sack.

It is a witch! She is very, very old and bent, dressed all in black. Her white hair is long and straggly, her nose is hooked, and she rides a broomstick. Her name is Befana and she, not Santa Claus, traditionally brings gifts to the children of Italy.

Befana pays her annual visit on January 6, the date when the Three Kings offered their gifts of gold, frankincense, and myrrh to the newborn Christ Child in Bethlehem.

In the weeks preceding Epiphany many youngsters write notes to Befana telling her the presents they would most like to receive. Girls and boys in Italy

The legend of La Befana

have to watch their manners as Epiphany nears. Befana knows what they have been up to and ill-behaved youngsters just might awaken on Epiphany morning to find a lump of coal in their stockings instead of candy and toys.

Befana's story begins at the time of the birth of Christ. According to legend, the Three Kings journeyed through Italy on their way to Bethlehem to worship the Christ Child. They stopped to ask directions of an old woman who was sweeping out her cottage, and they invited her to join them.

"I can't," she snapped gruffly. "I'm much too busy. And I've never heard of Bethlehem."

So the caravan moved on, the old woman staring thoughtfully after it. Shaking her head, she returned to her sweeping, trying to put the exotic travelers out of her mind. But she was lonely. Her husband had died long years before. She had always loved children and often wished she had some around to keep her company. Now there was a very special Child, far away in some place called Bethlehem. Wherever that was.

"I'll go after all! she cried. "If I hurry, perhaps I can catch up with them. I want to see the Christ Child, too, and bring Him a gift!"

And so she set out with her broom and a sack of goodies for the Infant Jesus. The way was long and difficult, and the old woman soon was lost. She never did find the caravan, nor did she reach Bethlehem. Yet, the story relates, she never gave up trying to find the Christ Child. Befana still searches, even today, even after all these centuries.

Whenever she comes to a house where there is a child, she drops in to see if it might be the one she seeks. It never is, but she leaves a gift, anyway. For Befana has come to realize, over the years, that her searching is not in vain, that in a way the Christ Child can be found in all children.

In recent years, Santa Claus, too, has become a popular figure in Italy. Called *Babbo Natale*, or Father Christmas, he has replaced the Befana in many parts of the country. But Befana has been delivering her gifts for almost 2,000 years. Most likely, she'll keep on doing it for many more.

Traditionally, Italian children receive their holiday gifts from an ugly old witch, called Befana. Here a Befana doll in colorful native costume watches passers-by from a market stall in the Piazza Navona in Rome.

Nunzia Falco's (age thirteen) interpretation of Befana's yearly visit (right). Instead of coming down the chimney, Befana saves time by dropping her gifts as she flies swiftly through the night sky on her broomstick.

23

The lovely story of Christ's birth has inspired countless artists through the centuries. In Italy, where religion has always played such an important role, representations of the Nativity have been created in many forms: in paintings and sculpture, mosaics and enamel, and in stained glass windows.

Manuscript illuminators, too, used the theme in ornamental initials at the start of a chapter, in border designs, or for full-page illustrations. These glowing, colorful scenes often gleamed with added touches of gold and silver. An example of illumination may be seen on the facing page. It shows Mary, Joseph, and the Infant Jesus in the stable, watched over by animals and angels in the background.

Christmas art

Nativity portrayals during the first few hundred years of the Christian era were rare. A few were carved on the walls of the catacombs beneath Rome, where the early Christians hid from their persecutors. One relief (a projection of figures on a flat surface) shows the Christ Child in His crib, with shepherds and the Three Kings nearby.

In later years, Italy's greatest artists and sculptors often chose Biblical themes for their work. In the 1200's, the Pisano family of sculptors included the Nativity in carved panels for churches. In the 1300's, the Florentine painter and sculptor Giotto portrayed the Madonna and Child, Joseph, shepherds, and angels in some of his frescoes (paintings on wet plaster).

During the early Renaissance (in the 1400's) the della Robbia family depicted the manger scene in some of their richly colored terra cotta (ceramic clay) medallions, used as architectural ornaments. Fra Angelico, Botticelli, Michelangelo, Tintoretto, and many others painted the Madonna and Child and other Biblical scenes such as the flight into Egypt or the shepherds and Wise Men worshipping at Christ's manger.

Neapolitan sculptors in the 1600's and 1700's retold the ancient Christmas story with their marvelous miniature figures and settings for the presepi, or manger scenes. Even today there are superb woodcarvers and makers of beautiful papier mâché figures who carry on the great tradition.

Italy's glassmakers have been masters of their trade for centuries, creating clear or colored goblets, vases, bowls, and beads. Venetian glass, manufactured in family-owned shops on the island of Murano, is famous the world over. When the Christmas tree became popular in Italy, the glassblowers turned their talents toward making ornaments and created a new form of Christmas art. The fragile glass balls, stars, and other shapes sometimes have a lacy pattern running through them; others may be transparent with a tiny object inside. Still others are adorned with designs or textured surfaces. All are exquisite—some of the loveliest ornaments to be found anywhere.

A Nativity scene (left) portrayed in a sculptured disk created in Milan around 1400. (Above) Shown is the Holy Family in the stable at Bethlehem, a fresco by Fra Angelico, famed Dominican friar and painter. (Right) Another Nativity scene, this one was created by Giovanni della Robbia of the celebrated Florentine family of sculptors. The figures are composed of ceramic clay (terra cotta) and highly glazed in glowing colors.

The joy of Christmas is not portrayed only by great masters and skilled craftsmen, however. There are the delightful homemade manger scenes lovingly fashioned of simple materials with a great deal of ingenuity and artistry. And there are the drawings made by Italian children at home or in school. All the many aspects of the Christmas season in Italy come to vivid life in these paintings: manger scenes, Christmas trees, presents, holiday meals with the family, and winter landscapes. Children's Christmas art is perhaps the most charming of all—colorful, honest, and endearing.

(Left, top to bottom) *Four paintings on the theme "Christmas in My Country" by Italian children: Ciro Ossorio, age ten; Giovanni Marra, age seven; Paolo Petrarolo, age ten; Stefano Limontini, age ten.*

(Right) *These beautiful Venetian glass Christmas ornaments are made on the island of Murano, where Italian glass blowers have been practicing their art for centuries.*

It was the winter of 1223. Christmas was coming, and a man named Francis was busily preparing a novel celebration near Assisi, high in the snow-covered Umbrian hills.

Francis (later Saint Francis) was born in 1182, the son of a wealthy Assisi merchant. As a youth, he had thoroughly enjoyed the good things money and position could bring. At age twenty, he became a soldier and was captured. During his imprisonment he fell ill, and believed that he heard voices. They told him he must change his way of life, give up his possessions, and go out into the world to preach the words of Christ.

Francis obeyed. He devoted himself to helping lepers and other outcasts, and he worked at restoring ruined churches. Barefoot and in rags he traveled to far-distant lands including Palestine, where he visited the birthplace of Christ.

The fabulous Italian mangers

Francis was a remarkable man, holy, humble, yet full of joy and bursting with eagerness to share his beliefs. He once wrote that he wished he could speak to the emperor. He would, he said, request that Christmas be shared by all, even the birds and other animals. Crumbs should be scattered on all the roadways on the anniversary of Jesus' birth, oxen and donkeys should be given an extra ration of food.

But his greatest desire was that people, all people, might share his wonder at the miracle of the birth of Christ. He wanted his followers to witness the story as it really had happened, to show them that Christ came from simple beginnings, just as they did.

So, Francis sent a message to Giovanni Vellita, a noble lord of the region. Vellita, who greatly respected Francis, came as fast as he could. He was a rather fat man, and he arrived huffing and puffing, red-faced from the exertion.

"What can I do for you, my friend?" Vellita wheezed.

"I want you to help arrange a celebration," Francis told him. "I would like to show how the Infant Jesus was born in Bethlehem, how He suffered from cold and lack of proper shelter, and how He lay in the manger warmed only by the breath of the ox and ass."

Vellita was delighted with the plan. He provided a manger filled with hay—and live animals, too. All the people of the countryside were invited, and they came carrying torchlights and candles. The friars sang hymns as Francis celebrated the Mass under the stars that Christmas Eve. In his own words, he related the old, old story of Jesus' birth.

As he spoke, the shepherds came, and Mary and Joseph, acted by real people. There were sheep, too, and an ass and an ox. The watchers must have felt that they had been transported back in time—more than 1,200 years—to that original manger scene. Francis gently placed a small wax figure of Jesus in the manger. He was so moved by the beauty of it all that he wept with joy.

Francis died in 1226. Two years later, he was declared a saint and eventually was named patron saint of all Italy. His small group of monks became the Franciscan order of the Roman Catholic Church.

St. Francis talking to the birds, a miniature from a thirteenth-century psalmbook (left). A sculptured manger scene in a church in Greccio (above) portrays St. Francis celebrating Christmas Mass in one niche and his reenactment of Christ's birth in Bethlehem in another.

One of the incredibly detailed Neapolitan presepi, this manger scene includes hundreds of miniature figures. It portrays not only the story of Christ's birth but also includes fascinating glimpses of life in old Naples. (Left) Musicians play their instruments as the Three Kings progress on their way to worship the Christ Child. (Right) Angels soar overhead as the Three Kings offer their wondrous gifts to the Infant Jesus in His manger.

(Left) *Here is another view of the presepio, with a castle in the background and, on the side, a portion of a Neapolitan tenement.* (Right) *In this section, a lively street scene is shown, complete with hanging meats and cheeses, and a tail-wagging dog wandering by.*

And his modest little reenactment of the Gospel story grew into a Christmas tradition beloved not only in Italy, but in many other countries around the world. It is called a *crèche* in French, *nacimiento* in Spanish. In Italian, it is the *presepio,* meaning "manger" or "crib."

The participants in the first live presepio enjoyed it so much that they repeated it year after year. Soon other towns took it up—and the custom spread. And someone, somewhere, had the idea of creating a presepio using small, carved figures. One of the earliest known manger scenes of this type appeared around the end of the 1200s, in Rome's Church of Santa Maria Maggiore. It still exists today.

At first, the scenes were simple and included only the Babe, Joseph, and Mary. Figures were usually crude, made of wood or clay. In the mid-1600s, the nobility became captivated by the presepi. The best artists available were commissioned to produce mangers, but now they were no longer merely Nativity groupings. Other Biblical tales were added, and the background began to portray typical Italian scenes, complete with bustling, crowded streets, or sheep-dotted mountainsides.

The Spanish Prince Charles of Bourbon became king of Naples in 1734, as Charles IV. He was fascinated by the miniature reproductions and enjoyed designing elaborate settings for them. Some say he even carved a few of the figures himself. His queen, Maria Amalia, sewed exquisite costumes for the figures with her own hands, as did her ladies in waiting. They used lace and rich fabrics, real jewels, and gold and silver.

By the late 1700s, the Neapolitan presepi reached heights of splendor and intricacy that have never since been equaled. Noble lords and ladies visited each other's houses to compare the lavish productions. A manger sometimes would occupy an entire room or even sprawl into adjacent rooms. The settings and figures were objects of religious devotion, to be sure, but they were also enchanting toys.

The tiny figures were completely realistic, down to the last wrinkle or wart, tiny vegetable or fruit, lantern or musical instrument. Each small human was dressed according to occupation or rank and in the fashion of the times: from great ladies and gentlemen down to the humblest villager. Men sat in a tavern drinking wine and twirling spaghetti on forks. Housewives haggled with vendors or wearily swept their doorsteps. Animals wandered amiably through the streets, a donkey lay down and rolled in the grass, a cow scratched with her hind leg.

Real waterfalls tumbled down rocky hillsides, and fountains gushed real water. In some presepi, Mount Vesuvius could be seen erupting in the background. So cleverly put together were the panoramas that it seemed as though the figures actually moved, breathed, sang, argued, ate, and drank. The scenes were fantastic and exuberant—vividly authentic reproductions of Neapolitan life, and masterpieces of the sculptor's art.

Fortunately, many of those magnificent, centuries-old presepi may still be seen. Some are on permanent display in museums or are reassembled at Christmastime in the great churches of Italy. King Charles' splendid exhibit, with 1,200 individual pieces, is in the Royal Palace of Caserta.

In Rome, one of the most impressive Christmas cribs may be visited at the Basilica of Saints Cosmos and Damian, near the Coliseum. It was created more than 200 years ago in Naples. Forty-five feet long, twenty-one feet wide, and twenty-seven feet high, it contains hundreds of hand-carved wooden figures.

Rome has the most famous Christ Child, too, the revered Santo Bambino, in the Church of Santa Maria in Ara Coeli. The little image is encrusted with precious jewels; its lifelike coloring is supposed to have been added by angels' hands. According to legend, a monk carved it of wood from the Mount of Olives in the Holy Land. The figure is believed to have miraculous healing powers. Once it was stolen, the story goes, but managed to return all by itself, waking up the friars by ringing the church bells and knocking loudly on the door. Supposedly, the small figure scolded them for having been so careless.

Still another view of the presepio: here a fiddler plays while the tavernkeeper brings a platter of food for his guests. Every detail is as perfect as the artist could make it, including the clothes worn by the participants and the expressions on their faces.

Believers write letters to the image, asking for special graces. The mail is always delivered, even if the address is only "Bambino, Roma." Every Christmas Eve the little figure is taken from its niche and placed into a splendid manger within the church. A platform is erected before it, where Roman children stand to deliver short sermons or sing. They are seldom shy about performing, speaking out with dramatic aplomb, often adding an encore at the slightest sign of encouragement.

In some regions, there are animated presepi, usually with large, almost life-size, figures. In Milan, one is erected in a structure next to the Duomo. It is hard to know where to begin looking: on one side a woodsman cuts a tree, by the river two fishermen haul out their catch. Washerwomen farther upstream pound and scrub their laundry, while children in a village chase chickens and dogs. On a small lake, a sailboat bounces on the choppy waves, and skiers swoop down snow-clad mountains in the background. Even the lighting changes, from sunny to cloudy to dusky, and then the moon and stars appear.

"Living" mangers are popular, too, with live participants portraying the various characters in the Nativity tale. They are like Saint Francis' reenactment, but with more people. In Rivisondoli, in the rugged mountains of Abruzzi, a living presepio is put on each year. The entire village participates in the show, and there may be as many as 600 actors. Others join in, too: vacationers who have come for the skiing often sign up for coveted roles, especially that of the Virgin.

Preparations begin weeks in advance with rounding up as many people as possible who own one of the beautiful regional costumes. Animals, too, are needed. The actors do not get paid for performing, but the animals—or, rather, their owners—do. The show begins in the late afternoon of January 5, and huge crowds gather to watch.

Rivisondoli lies at an altitude of almost 4,000 feet. At this time of year, the ground is usually deep in snow, and often more snow is falling. It is dark, but spotlights from below trace the actors' path as they move slowly down the mountainside. There are

At the left, is the revered Gesú Bambino, the bejeweled image of the Christ Child in Rome's Church of Santa Maria in Ara Coeli. The Bambino rests in His niche above the altar as Christmas Mass begins (above left). During the Mass the Bambino is carried in a procession through the church and then placed into His manger (above right).

shepherds galore, mostly real ones, as this is a region of shepherds. Some of the villagers bring gifts — fruit, live chickens, pigs or lambs — for the Infant Jesus. The Three Kings ride down on horses. To play a king is a very great honor, so the roles are customarily allotted to the mayors of nearby villages.

Finally, Mary appears astride a donkey. She carries a real baby, and Joseph walks proudly at her side. Sheep mill about in large numbers; an ox and ass stand patiently waiting. It is a colorful, moving spectacle, ending at a humble manger set inside a shallow cave, as all the players gather 'round and sing.

After its peak in the seventeenth and eighteenth centuries, the practice of creating enormous, costly presepi almost died out. But in this century, interest in the manger scenes sprang up again. And at Christmastime today it seems as though all of Italy is

Two scenes from a "living presepio" are shown here. (Above top) *The villagers of Sassi portray the Biblical roles in their reenactment of the story of Christ's birth. The procession comes down the steps of this mountain village and ends inside the door to the right, cut into the rock.* (Below) *The actors gather around a real infant as they act out the ancient tale. In the foreground are gifts of bread and wine, which the townsfolk have brought for the Christ Child.*

one giant presepio. There is even a worldwide organization called Friends of the Presepio that works constantly to preserve the mangers of the past and to promote the art of making new ones.

Contests for the best crib displays are held throughout the country, in schools, places of business, and town halls. Nativity scenes are erected virtually everywhere—not only in homes and churches, villages and city squares, but in gas stations and post offices, airports, and railway depots. Shop windows offer unique versions, some made entirely of pastry and some carved out of butter. There are presepi made all of shells or seeds, bread dough, and even fruit.

Children make mangers as school projects, from cardboard, papier mâché or, in one case, from old bottles and used light bulbs. Smaller mangers are often installed inside old television sets. Like big shadow boxes, they offer depth for better perspective—and they are portable! Manger figures range from life-size to some so tiny that they fit into a nutshell.

The presepio is set up sometime during the weeks before Christmas. Most families purchase a few new figures at the market each year. Some markets sell nothing else. Presepi are like sets of electric trains—one never has enough pieces. Many families hand valuable figures down from generation to generation. Other presepi may be made of cardboard or plastic, but all are cherished in the same measure.

Until Christmas Eve, the manger lies empty. Then, with great ceremony, the Bambino is laid in His crib. Some households have two sets of the Three Kings: one reenacts their caravan journey, the second kneels before the manger. Other families move the little figures as the days pass, allowing the Kings to reach the stable exactly on January 6. On Epiphany or shortly after, the presepio is dismantled and carefully put away till next year.

The presepi of Italy may have changed through the years since Saint Francis' simple version. His affection for the original Nativity scene in Bethlehem, however, is still very much alive in the hearts of Italians today.

Dressed in regional costumes, villagers take part in another living manger scene in Rivisondoli, Abruzzi.

It is believed that the first church bells ever used in a Christian service were Italian, and that they pealed out on a Christmas Eve about 1,600 years ago. Until that time, the faithful had been called to Mass by a man going around the community ringing a handbell.

Bishop Paulinus of Nola, in the province of Campania, is credited with instituting the custom of using church bells, instead. Since then, the joyous clangor of bells has become associated with Christmas everywhere. And in Italy today, at midnight on Christmas Eve, all the country's churches ring out the glad tidings, "Christ is born!"

Music from the hills

Two generations of zampognari pipe their old shepherd tunes (above). A bagpiper's music makes the long climb to the Ara Coeli church seem easier (right).

The most characteristic Italian Christmas sound, however, is not that of bells, but of bagpipes. Sometime around the middle of December, the noisy market in Rome's Piazza Navona shrills with a new sound: the bagpipers have arrived!

Called *zampognari*, they are shepherds who live high in the mountains and come down each year at Christmastime to perform in the market and at other sites in Rome. They still visit other cities and towns, too, particularly in the regions of Calabria and Abruzzi. The melodies they play are adaptations of old hill tunes, such as the shepherd song, "Cantata dei Pastori."

Most people think of bagpipes as Scottish, but they have long been found in one form or another in many lands. In Italy, they go back to the ancient Romans. Legend says that shepherds, who traditionally play the bagpipes, entertained Mary in Bethlehem long ago. She supposedly preferred their strange, droning music to any other. One story claims that thoughtful shepherds even eased her labor pains with their melodies.

In years past, the zampognari made a practice of stopping before every shrine to the Madonna and every Nativity scene. There they would serenade the

Virgin Mother. They also paid visits to carpenters' shops to honor Joseph's memory.

In some regions, the zampognari and *pifferari*, "flutists," would go from door to door and knock. They would ask if the householder wished them to return for the novena, the nine days of special prayers before Christmas. If the answer was yes, they would leave a wooden spoon or mark the doorway in some manner.

When the musicians came back, they would gather to sing and play in front of the family's manger scene. Money or food was given in exchange for their services. In Sicily, the shepherds were often joined by a violinist and cellist.

Modern-day zampognari still dress much as their ancestors did, and they are a fascinating sight in their shaggy sheepskin vests, leather breeches, or sheepskin leggings. Over their shoulders they wear long woolen cloaks, and their white stockings are bound by leather thongs reaching up to the knees.

Once they walked all the way down from their mountain meadows; nowadays many drive or ride motor scooters. Their arrival is a cheerful announcement that Christmas is near.

A solitary bagpiper plays a Christmas melody in a misty Sicilian street.

Within the city of Rome lies another city: the Vatican. It extends over only about 108 acres, and its gardens, courtyards, and magnificent buildings are almost completely surrounded by walls. The museums and chapels of the Vatican Palace contain some of the world's greatest works of art. St. Peter's Basilica, looking out over a vast square, is the largest Christian church in the world. Headquarters of the Roman Catholic Church, the Vatican is also the official residence of the Pope.

Since 1968, the Pope has presided over a special ceremony for children on the last Sunday before Christmas. Thousands of youngsters bring their manger figure of Baby Jesus to St. Peter's Square to be blessed by the Pope. When John Paul II observed his first Christmas as Pope in 1978, more than 50,000 of Rome's schoolchildren came to the square. They serenaded John Paul with carols, including a Christmas song from his native Poland. The Pope was delighted. Energetically conducting from his balcony, he sang right along with the youngsters.

There has long been a special bond between Popes and Italy's beloved manger scenes. Pope Honorius III gave Saint Francis permission to create his live Nativity scene, the first ever, way back in 1223. Paul

Christmas
at the Vatican

VI, who became Pope in 1963, was particularly fond of mangers. He ordered a new one for the Mathilde Chapel in the Vatican and placed the figure of the Christ Child in the crib himself.

In 1965, a children's Christmas party was given at the Vatican. The young guests were all winners of local manger contests. A large presepio with a lovely blue sky and lots of flying angels had been set up in the background.

Paul VI entered the room and spoke to the children about the meaning of the Nativity scene. Then he invited them to sit down for the holiday meal, and, to the youngsters' astonishment, himself poured the soup into each child's bowl. After a festive lunch, the children offered the Pope a live lamb. They played some games, too, and sang carols. Finally, three tall men entered the room, dressed in the gorgeous costumes of the Three Kings. Behind them walked a solemn camel—a real one, borrowed from the Roman zoo! On the camel's back was a large bag full of gifts from the Pope. The children— and Paul VI, obviously—had a fine time.

Christmas in the Vatican is a splendid occasion, rich with pageantry, music, incense, glowing colors, and precious jewels. The highlight is Midnight Mass on Christmas Eve, celebrated by the Pope in St. Peter's. It is an incredibly impressive church, glittering with gold and filled with priceless paintings, statues, and mosaics. The main altar stands in the center, its bronze canopy upheld by massive, ornate columns. And more than 400 feet overhead looms the awesome dome, designed by Michelangelo.

Around 10 PM, the huge basilica slowly begins to fill with people. Photographers rush about busily preparing their cameras, setting up tripods, flashes, and floodlights. Television crews, too, bustle purposefully around their cameras mounted on movable scaffolds, trying out different angles and positions. The services on this night will be televised via satellite all around the world.

As the hour advances, the pace quickens. The crowds become larger and the people seem to move faster. There are nuns and priests, and seminarians in great numbers. There are tourists and pilgrims

A young boy (left) solemnly holds up his manger figure of the Christ Child to be blessed by the Pope. Every year thousands of children bring their little images to St. Peter's Square in Rome on the Sunday before Christmas for a special blessing. (Right) A Roman Christmas scene: a loving grandmother holds her warmly dressed, small grandchild.

from many lands — Africa, Australia, India, the Philippines. And there are Italians — young and old, rich and poor. The children, and there are many, are quite well behaved. Some move from one family member to another, trying to persuade someone to lift them up for a better view. Older boys and girls climb on columns or balustrades to see.

At 11 o'clock, the church is suddenly flooded with light and the music and the singing begin. Then, a sudden hush, followed by excited murmurs: "Here he comes!" Somebody has spotted the Pope. But first come the cardinals, the Swiss guards in their colorful medieval costumes, the bishops, and a large retinue of priests. Then the Pontiff appears, greeting and blessing the crowds on both sides of the aisle.

The Pope arrives at the altar and begins to celebrate the Mass. It is a long service, with much singing of chants followed by responses. The Pope delivers the sermon. He also personally gives Communion to several hundred worshipers. The rest of the multitude are served by his many assistants. Now the Mass is over, and the Pope again crosses the entire length of the basilica. Everyone applauds vigorously, shouting, *"Viva il Papa!"*

The Holy Father proceeds slowly, acknowledging the warm, emotional reception with smiles and blessings. Some high-ranking dignitaries follow him into the sacristy. The rest of the crowd gradually file out of the church, into the rainy Christmas morning.

Nuns follow the Mass in St. Peter's Church in the Vatican on Christmas Eve (left). Pope Paul VI celebrates Christmas Midnight Mass at the great central altar in St. Peter's (above).

There is no such thing as a "typical" Christmas menu in Italy. Traditional foods and methods of cooking vary widely throughout the country's twenty regions. They have one thing in common, though. They are all excellent.

Italian housewives make a point of choosing only the freshest ingredients for their kitchens. Several trips to the market are necessary, and the process of selection is taken seriously. It is accomplished usually with considerable discussion, sometimes loud, between wary purchaser and eager seller. Husbands often accompany their wives, offering critical advice as to which eel is the fattest, dismissing this pear or that artichoke as having too many spots. And that is only the beginning!

Holiday foods

Next come long hours of preparation: making pasta by hand, simmering sauces, creating an extravagant number of desserts, and much more. Each recipe is concocted with a generous hand, too—no skimping in Italian cooking. Some of the results will be shared with lucky friends and neighbors; the rest will disappear like magic during the holidays.

Many Italians observe a rigid twenty-four-hour fast that ends on Christmas Eve, so appetites are whetted to their sharpest on that night. The table is set with the family's finest linens, china, and silver. Even in the poorer homes this is the one time of the year when no one has to stint, when an elaborate banquet of all the traditional foods must be served. Some families have been known to pawn their furniture, or a wife's wedding ring, so as to ensure the proper quantity—and quality—of tempting courses.

The Christmas Eve meal begins around seven or eight o'clock and usually lasts for several hours. By ancient custom, it is meatless. In Naples and other parts of southern Italy, a large female eel, *capitone,* is served, with various sauces, as the main course. Capitoni are also popular in areas as far north as Chioggia, near Venice, where the best eels are bred. They are sold live at the market, and depending on the area or the family tradition, roasted, baked, fried, or steamed with rice. Along the seacoast, *calamari,* or squid, is the favored delicacy. *Vongoli,* small clams, are another common Christmas Eve offering, as is *baccalà,* codfish.

There will also be vegetables: some dipped in fritter batter and deep fried (*fritto misto*), beans of many kinds, and perhaps an assortment of vegetables pickled in vinegar. Salads, too, are served, and usually a colorful platter of antipasto. Crusty loaves of bread and pasta in countless shapes and sizes round out the meal, which is followed by sweets and *caffé espresso.* Wine always accompanies the supper, often ending with *Asti Spumanti,* Italy's champagne. Afterward, nearly everyone goes to Midnight Mass, well fed and ready to thoroughly enjoy the beautiful holy night services.

Others attend church the next morning, and Christmas dinner is served shortly after noon. In

Artistically arranged fruit displays (left) *add a brilliant touch of color to the many open-air Christmas markets. Bread making* (above top) *is an important part of holiday meal preparations, and it is still done in a primitive way in many areas of Italy.* (Below) *Seafood is traditionally served for Christmas Eve supper in Italy, and this Sicilian fish market offers a variety of selections.*

many families the children, using their best penmanship, write special letters for this occasion. The letters are then hidden somewhere on the table, under Papa's plate or perhaps tucked inside a napkin. In them, the youngsters ask forgiveness for any misdeeds they may have committed and promise to be very, very good in the coming year.

Papa pretends to see nothing unusual about the table, despite all the excited giggling going on. Suddenly he spies a not-too-well-concealed note.

"What's this?" he asks with a great show of astonishment. "A letter for Mama and me?"

He then proceeds to read the letter aloud, with much dramatic fervor. Mama beams, battling a tear or two of maternal pride. Grandparents utter cries of admiration, and even older brothers and sisters applaud the young ones' efforts.

Christmas dinner, like most Italian meals, starts off with soup—usually *tortellini in brodo* (broth). Tortellini, generally homemade, are little pasta casings stuffed with a spiced meat mixture. In Sicily,

These lacy cookies, an Italian Christmas specialty, are called pizzelle (top). *Preparing the dough for the Christmas treats* (bottom) *requires much time and patience.*

Crisp cookies are all ready for holiday nibbling. At top left are crostoli, and underneath are biscotti. An Italian housewife (above) adds a final touch of powdered sugar to her array of Christmas cookies.

roast turkey is preferred; in other regions, a baked, stuffed ham. Lentils with sausage will often appear as a side dish. Lentils may also be served on New Year's Day. Once they symbolized money, and in some areas even today it is believed that eating them will guarantee a year of prosperity and good luck.

A holiday dessert staple in almost every region of Italy nowadays is *panettone,* once found only in Milan. Made with currants and candied fruit, it is a yeast cake, very light and high, baked in a fluted pan and then glazed. Making panettone from scratch is a lengthy process, so most people buy a commercial brand. It is sold in almost every kind of shop and is a popular gift item at Christmastime.

Amaretti, almond macaroons, are favorite sweets, as are *cannoli,* crisp pastry shells filled with creamy ricotta cheese, whipped cream, and candied fruit. There are *strufoli,* too, little balls of dough fried in oil and as light as a feather. They are dipped in honey, sprinkled with colored sugar beads, and eaten with the fingers.

Delicate sweets called *pinocchiati,* made with pine nuts, are a central Italian specialty, particularly in the region of Umbria. The province of Siena invented spicy *panforte* back in the Middle Ages. Today it is available all over the country. It is more candy than cake, solid with fruit and nuts, and very chewy.

Sicilian cooks are renowned for their delectable desserts, and their masterpiece is the luscious *cassata,* a sponge cake with a filling of ricotta, candied fruit, almonds, grated chocolate, and rum.

Fruit, nuts, and candy are always offered at the end of the meal. Sweets and fruit, now served so lavishly, were once a very special treat in Italy. Often Christmas was the only time of the year when one could afford to eat them.

A great many Italian candies and desserts are made with nuts and honey. The people once believed that nuts could ensure fertile fields, flocks, and families. And in the time of the ancient Romans, honey was thought to have almost magical properties. It was often given as a present, especially at New Year's, so that "the coming year would be as sweet as the gift."

A mouth-watering display of Italian holiday foods . . .

A gaily-trimmed Christmas tree stands in a quiet square in Rome.

The holiday season in Italy is a happy time, rich with religious feeling and spiced with lavish quantities of good things to eat. On the following pages you will find recipes for typical dishes and sweets from many regions, so that you can create your own authentic Italian Christmas feast.

Decorating the house is an important part of holiday fun in Italy, too. Quilling is one of the country's many delightful folk arts, and we have included easy-to-follow directions for making a charming quilled tree ornament. You will also find another enjoyable project for the whole family: a paper version of a stained glass window.

Italy is a land of song, and no Italian Christmas would be complete without music. We have chosen three traditional carols, including a Sicilian bagpipers' melody, the lovely "Jesus, The Newborn Baby," and the ever popular "From Starry Skies Thou Comest," written and composed by Saint Alphonsus Liguori.

A festively decorated house filled with family, friends, and song, and a holiday table laden with delicious food—that's an Italian Christmas. We wish you and yours *Buon Natale!*

From Italy, a very merry Christmas

Holiday treats

Lentils with sausage

1 cup lentils, rinsed
2 cups water
1 cup dry white wine
2 tablespoons olive oil
1 large tomato, peeled, seeded, and chopped
1 slice bacon, diced
1 clove garlic, chopped
3 peppercorns
1 small bay leaf
Salt to taste
2 pounds mild Italian sausage
1 small onion
1 small carrot, diced
1 stalk celery, cut in pieces
4 peppercorns
1 small bay leaf

1. Combine lentils, water, wine, oil, tomato, bacon, garlic, 3 peppercorns, 1 bay leaf, and salt in a saucepan. Bring to boil, reduce heat, and simmer covered about 1 hour, or until lentils are soft.
2. Meanwhile, put sausage, onion, carrot, celery, and remaining peppercorns and bay leaf into a large saucepan. Add enough water to cover by 1 inch. Bring to boil, reduce heat, and simmer covered 30 minutes. Remove sausage from liquid, remove casing, and cut into thick slices.
3. Serve sausage slices with lentils.
    4 servings

Baked cod

2 pounds salted cod, cut in serving pieces
1 can (16 ounces) tomatoes, drained and sieved
¼ cup chopped green olives
2 tablespoons capers
1 tablespoon snipped parsley
½ teaspoon salt
¼ teaspoon pepper
½ teaspoon oregano

1. Soak salted cod in cold water 24 hours, changing water every few hours.
2. Rinse with cold water, and pat dry. Arrange pieces in a greased 2-quart baking dish.
3. Combine sieved tomatoes, olives, capers, parsley, and seasonings in a saucepan. Bring to boil. Pour sauce over fish.
4. Bake at 350°F. 25 to 30 minutes, or until fish flakes easily when tested with a fork.

Fried eel

2½ pounds eels, cleaned and dried
½ cup flour
Salt and pepper to taste
1 teaspoon rosemary
⅓ cup olive oil
Lemon slices

1. Cut eels crosswise into 3-inch pieces. Coat with flour and season with salt, pepper, and rosemary.
2. Heat oil in a skillet. Add coated eel pieces and fry over medium heat until golden brown on both sides (about 10 minutes).
3. Accompany eel with lemon slices.
   6 servings

Spaghetti with tuna

⅓ cup olive oil
⅓ cup butter
1 can (6½ or 7 ounces) tuna, drained and flaked
¼ cup snipped parsley
3 tablespoons water
1 pound spaghetti, cooked following package
   directions

1. Put oil, butter, tuna, and parsley into a small saucepan. Set over low heat for 3 or 4 minutes. Stir well. Add water and simmer 10 minutes.
2. Combine hot spaghetti and sauce and serve immediately.
   6 servings

Mixed fry of vegetables

1 small eggplant, pared
4 small zucchini
Salt
1 cup flour
¼ teaspoon salt
3 tablespoons olive oil
¾ cup warm water
4 ounces mozzarella
1 egg white
Oil for frying

1. Cut eggplant in half crosswise, then cut lengthwise into 3-inch sticks. Cut zucchini into lengthwise sticks. Sprinkle salt over vegetables and allow to stand about 2 hours. Drain off liquid.
2. Put flour and ¼ teaspoon salt into a bowl, add oil and water, and stir until smooth. Set aside 2 hours.
3. Slice cheese about ⅛-inch thick and cut into 3-inch lengths.
4. Heat a ½-inch depth of oil in a large skillet. If desired, use 2 skillets.
5. Just before using batter, beat egg white until soft peaks are formed and fold into batter until blended.
6. Dip some of the vegetable and cheese pieces into batter, then fry, a layer at a time, in hot oil until browned, turning as necessary. Drain on absorbent paper.
   6 servings

Cannoli

Filling:
2 pounds ricotta
2 teaspoons vanilla extract
½ cup confectioners' sugar
½ cup finely chopped candied citron
½ cup semisweet chocolate pieces

Shells:
3 cups flour
¼ cup sugar
1 teaspoon cinnamon
¼ teaspoon salt
3 tablespoons shortening
2 eggs, well beaten
2 tablespoons white vinegar
2 tablespoons cold water
Oil for deep frying
1 egg white, slightly beaten
¼ to ½ cup finely chopped blanched pistachio nuts
Sifted confectioners' sugar

1. To make filling, beat cheese with vanilla extract. Add ½ cup confectioners' sugar and beat until smooth. Fold in candied citron and chocolate pieces. Chill thoroughly.

2. To make shells, combine flour, sugar, cinnamon, and salt. Using a pastry blender, cut in shortening until pieces are the size of small peas. Stir in eggs; blend in vinegar and cold water.

3. Turn dough onto a lightly floured surface and knead until smooth and elastic (5 to 10 minutes). Wrap in waxed paper and chill 30 minutes.

4. Fill a deep saucepan a little over half full with oil. Heat oil slowly to 360°F.

5. Roll out chilled dough ⅛ inch thick. Using a 6×4½-inch oval pattern cut from cardboard, cut ovals from dough with a pastry cutter or sharp knife.

6. Wrap dough loosely around cannoli tubes (see Note), just lapping over opposite edge. Brush overlapping edges with egg white and press together to seal.

7. Fry shells in hot oil about 8 minutes, or until golden brown, turning occasionally. Fry only a few at a time, being careful not to crowd them. Using a slotted spoon or tongs, remove from oil, and drain over pan before removing to absorbent paper. Cool slightly and remove tubes. Cool completely.

8. When ready to serve, fill shells with ricotta filling. Sprinkle ends of filled shells with pistachio nuts and dust shells generously with confectioners' sugar.

About 16 filled rolls

Note: Aluminum cannoli tubes or clean, unpainted wooden sticks, 6 inches long and ¾ inch in diameter, may be used.

Strufoli

1¾ to 2 cups flour
¼ teaspoon salt
3 eggs
½ teaspoon vanilla extract
1 cup honey
1 tablespoon sugar
2 tablespoons grated orange peel (optional)
Oil for deep frying
1 tablespoon tiny multicolored candies

1. Put 1 cup flour and salt into a medium bowl. Make a well in center and add 1 egg at a time, mixing slightly after each addition. Add vanilla extract. Stir in more of the flour to make a soft dough.
2. Turn dough onto a floured surface and knead until dough is smooth and elastic. Cover and let stand about 30 minutes.
3. Divide dough into halves. Lightly roll each half into a rectangle ¼-inch thick; cut into strips ¼-inch wide. Use palm of hand to roll strips to pencil thickness. Cut into pieces about ¼- to ½-inch long.
4. Fill a deep saucepan a little over half full with oil; heat slowly to 375°F.
5. Put honey and sugar into a small (3-cup) skillet; place over low heat about 5 minutes. Stir in orange peel. Set aside but keep warm.
6. Add only as many pieces of dough at a time to hot oil as will float one layer deep. Fry 3 to 5 minutes, or until lightly browned, turning as necessary. Drain on absorbent paper.
7. Add hot cooked pieces to warm honey; stir until they are coated with syrup, then lift out with a slotted spoon or fork and put on a foil-covered tray.
8. Refrigerate until slightly chilled. Arrange in a conical shape on a serving plate: Invert a small custard cup at center of plate and pile the coated pieces over and around it. Sprinkle the tiny candies over the top.
9. To serve, spoon apart in clusters.
   8 to 10 servings

Almond macaroons

1 can (8 ounces) almond paste, cut in pieces
1 cup plus 2 tablespoons sugar
2 egg whites
Pine nuts

1. Combine almond paste, sugar, and egg whites in a bowl and work with a spoon until smooth.
2. Drop by teaspoonfuls onto cookie sheets lined with unglazed paper. Top with pine nuts.
3. Bake at 325°F. about 12 minutes, or until delicately browned. Cool slightly, then remove cookies to racks to cool.
   About 3 dozen cookies

Festive decorations

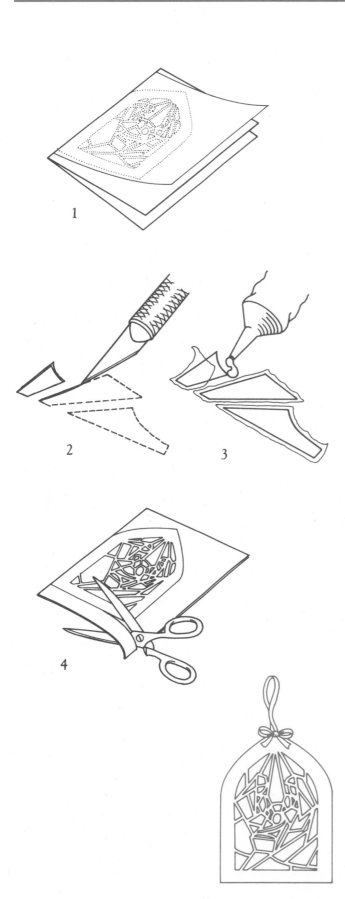

Stained glass window

1. Trace pattern onto lightweight paper. Rub back side of pattern with a white drawing pencil or chalk. Then fold in half a sheet of black construction paper or similar paper. Position the traced pattern over the folded sheet with the pattern beginning at the edge of the fold, and trace over the pattern again, using sufficient pressure to leave a white pattern line on top of the folded black sheet.

2. Tape the folded sheet to a cutting surface. Using a small hobby knife, cut out the areas that represent the different panes of stained glass, making sure to cut through both black thicknesses at the same time. Do not cut window's outer edges yet.

3. Following the color scheme, cut out pieces of tissue paper to fill the panes. To allow for gluing surface, make sure each piece is slightly larger than the area to be filled. Unfold the black sheet. Working at the inner surface of one window, glue the tissue pieces into place along the black lines that border each pane of stained glass.

Now glue the two halves of folded black paper together, applying glue lightly only to the black dividing lines and to the larger black areas around the edges. Do not spill glue on the tissue paper, through which the light will pass.

4. When the glue is dry, cut out the window itself. During the day, display the decoration in front of a sunny window. Otherwise, place in front of any available light source.

Window pattern

Colors: **A** Blue
B Yellow
C Red
D White
E Orange
F Violet
G Light green
H Dark green

71

Quilled star

1. Trace complete design on lightweight paper. Lay paper pattern on a piece of corrugated cardboard. Tape a sheet of wax paper over pattern.

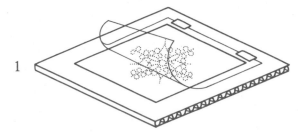

1

2. Cut red and yellow construction paper into ¼" strips of the following lengths: RED—four 5" strips and four 6" strips; YELLOW—seventeen 3" strips and eight 5" strips. Substitute other colors if desired. Curl these shapes:

Tight Rolls Use eight 3" yellow strips. Moisten one end and, beginning with this end, roll the paper around the center of a toothpick. Keep paper tight as you roll. Glue loose end into place and hold until glue is dry. Carefully remove toothpick.

Loose Roll Use one 3" yellow strip. Roll as for tight roll, then let roll unwind a bit. Glue loose end.

Marquise Use four 6" red strips to make four loose rolls. Pinch each roll on either side to form an eye shape.

Scroll Shapes Use eight 3" yellow strips. Loosely roll both ends of each strip towards the center, but not all the way to the center.

"V" Shapes Use eight 5" yellow strips. Pinch each strip in the center, forming a V. Then roll ends loosely outward.

Heart Shapes Use four 5" red strips. Pinch in center as for "V" shape, but roll ends inward to form a heart shape.

2

3. Arrange shapes, a few at a time, starting in the center and working out on wax paper over pattern.

4. With a toothpick, apply a dab of glue at each connecting point. While glue dries, anchor shapes with stick pins wherever necessary to bend and hold shapes in place. Remove pins when glue is completely dry. For hanging, attach looped thread.

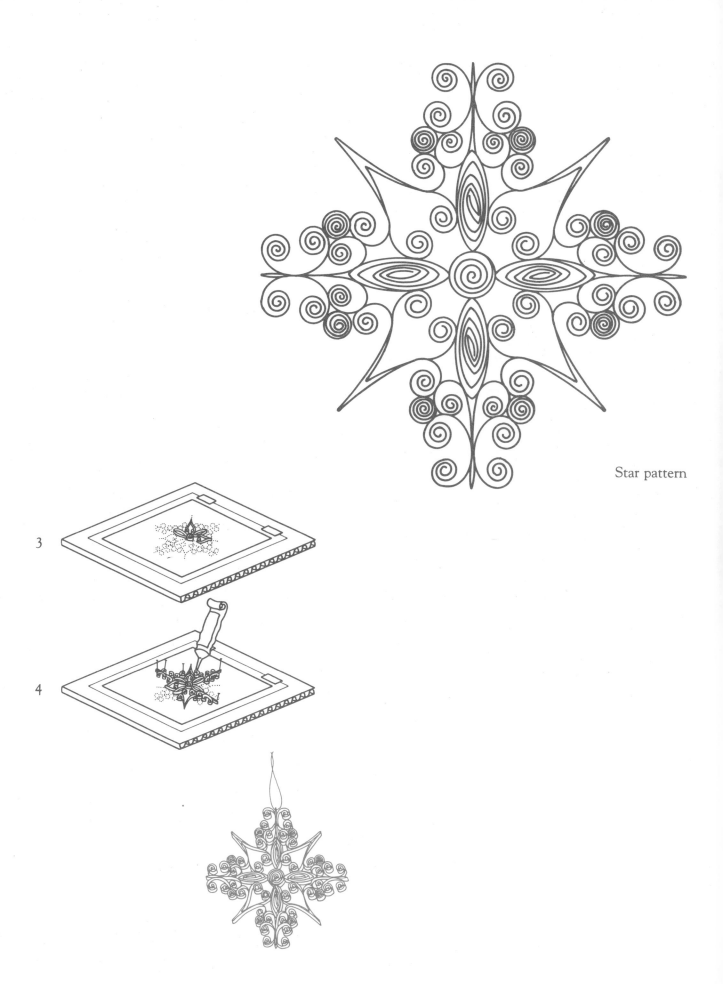

Star pattern

3

4

Christmas tunes

Carol of The Bagpipers

Traditional Sicilian
Translation: Dr. Theodore Baker, 1904

1. Quan - no na - scet - te Nin - no a Bet - te - lem - me,___ E -
1. When Christ our Lord was born___ at Beth - le - hem a - far,___ Al -

ra ___ not - te e pa - re - a mie - zo jour -
though 'twas night, there shone___ as___ bright as noon, a

Walter Ehret, George K. Evans, *The International Book of Christmas Carols*, © 1963, pp 242-250. Reprinted by permission of Prentice-Hall, Inc., Englewood Cliffs, New Jersey.

no. *Ma - je le stel - le, lu - ste - re_e bel - le, Se__ ve -*
star. Nev - er so bright - ly, nev - er so white - ly, Shone__ the

det - te - ro ac - cu - sì! La chiù lu - cen__ te__ Jet -
stars,__ as on__ that night! The bright - est star__ went__ A

te_a chiam - mà li Ma - gi, in O - ri - en - te.__
way to call the Wise__ Men__ from the O - ri - ent.__

From Starry Skies Thou Comest

Alphonsus Liguori (1696-1787)

Andante

1. Tu scen - di dal - le stel - le O Re del Cie -
1. From star - ry skies Thou com - est, The King_ of Heav'n fore-

lo_____ E vie - ni in u - na grot - ta Al
told,_____ Ap - pear - ing in a man - ger, Near

fred-do al ge - lo O Bam - bi - no mio Di - vi - no Io Ti
fro - zen from_the cold. Je - sus, dear-est lit - tle Ba - by, How I

ve - do qui tre - mar!____ O Di - o be-a - to!____ Oh
long to make Thee warm!____ To shel - ter Thee_from harm!____ My

quan - to Ti co - stò l'a - ver-mi a-ma - to!____
heart is filled with pit - y For Thy ti - ny form!____

2. *A te, che sei del mondo*
   Il creatore,
   Mancano panni e fuoco,
   O mio Signore.
   Caro, eletto pargoletto,
   Quanto questa poverta
   Piu m'innamora,
   Giacche ti fece amor povero ancora.

2. In Heav'n Thou wert Creator,
   The True and Only Word,
   Yet here on earth no fire, Lord,
   To keep Thee from the cold.
   Jesus, dearest little baby,
   Come in direst poverty,
   Would I had gifts for Thee!
   How wonderful God's love that suffers
       here for me!

Jesus, The Newborn Baby

Traditional Italian

Andante

1. Ge - sù Bam - bin l'e na - to, _____ Na - to in Be - te -
1. Je - sus, the new-born Ba - by, _____ Lies here in Beth - le -

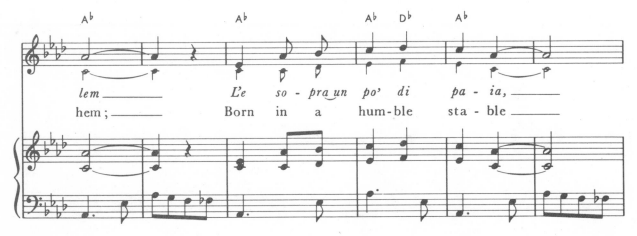

lem _____ L'e so - pra un po' di pa - ia, _____
hem; _____ Born in a hum - ble sta - ble _____

So - pra un po'___ di fien,___ L'e so - pra un po' di
Is Heav - en's pre - cious Gem.___ He is a pre - cious

fien S'a j'e'l bam - bin ch'a piu - ra, Soa ma - ma ch'a lo a -
Gem, Al - though we find Him cry - ing! In Ma - ry's arms He's

do - ra,___ L'e so - pra un po'___ di fien.___
sigh - ing,___ Je - sus, our Di - a - dem.___

2. *Assent na vôs ant l'aira,*
   Assent a vuì ciantand;
   L'è San Giusep so paire
   Lo pija 'ntii so brass!
   S'ai cianta la canssôn,
   Larin, larin, lareta,
   Gloria in Excelsis Deo,
   Tut a l'ônôr 'd l'anfan!

2. We hear a sweet voice singing
   Songs for the Holy One,
   Joseph, the Baby's father,
   Nestles Him close and warm.
   "Loo, loo, my dearest Son."
   O see, 'tis Joseph crooning,
   His tiny Baby soothing!
   Glory to God's own Son!

Illustration acknowledgements

Cover: Photo by Dean Jacobson
2: © Michael A. Vaccaro from Louis Mercier
6: Kinuko Craft
8: © Mark Roth
9: Vezio Sabatini,
Marka Graphic Photos & Archivium
10: Bernard Arendt
11: World Book photo by Jadwiga Lopez
13: © Marcella Pedone
14: Angelo Novi, Black Star
16: World Book photos by Jadwiga Lopez
17: © Michael A. Vaccaro from Louis Mercier
19: (top) World Book photo by Jadwiga Lopez,
(bottom) Robert Knopes, Nancy Palmer
Photo Agency, Inc.
20: World Book photo by Jadwiga Lopez
22: World Book photo by Jadwiga Lopez
23: Painting by Nunzia Falco from Christian
Children's Fund, Inc.
24: Courtesy of L'Italia
26: Marka Graphic Photos & Archivium
27: Gaetano Barone
28: (top to bottom) Paintings by Italian
children, courtesy of International
Collection of Child Art, Ewing Museum of
Nations, Illinois State University,
Normal, Illinois
29: World Book photo by Steve Hale
30: © Michael A. Vaccaro from Louis Mercier
33: (top) Historical Pictures Service, Inc.,
(bottom) Gaetano Barone
34: © Giuseppe De Pietro
35: © Giuseppe De Pietro
36: © Giuseppe De Pietro
38: © Michael A. Vaccaro from Louis Mercier
39: (left) © John G. Ross,
(right) © Giuseppe De Pietro
40-41: World Book photo by Steve Hale
42: © Marcella Pedone
43: © Marcella Pedone
44: © Vittorugo Contino
46: © Michael A. Vaccaro from Louis Mercier
47: World Book photo by Jadwiga Lopez
48: © Vittorugo Contino
50: © Michael A. Vaccaro from Louis Mercier
52: World Book photo by Jadwiga Lopez
53: © Michael A. Vaccaro from Louis Mercier
54: © Nicholas Devore III, Bruce Coleman Inc.
55: © Nicholas Devore III, Bruce Coleman Inc.
58: © Giuseppe De Pietro
59: © Marcella Pedone
60: Bernard Arendt
61: Bernard Arendt
63: Bob Scott Studio Inc.
64: © Nicholas Devore III, Bruce Coleman Inc.
70-73: Kathy Clo